Temptation Sensation

ADULT POETRY

PINK LEMONADE

authorHOUSE®

AuthorHouse™
1663 Liberty Drive
Bloomington, IN 47403
www.authorhouse.com
Phone: 833-262-8899

Published by AuthorHouse 12/10/2020

ISBN: 978-1-6655-1024-0 (sc)
ISBN: 978-1-6655-1023-3 (e)

Print information available on the last page.

Any people depicted in stock imagery provided by Getty Images are models, and such images are being used for illustrative purposes only. Certain stock imagery © Getty Images.

This book is printed on acid-free paper.

Because of the dynamic nature of the Internet, any web addresses or links contained in this book may have changed since publication and may no longer be valid. The views expressed in this work are solely those of the author and do not necessarily reflect the views of the publisher, and the publisher hereby disclaims any responsibility for them.

Contents

Dedication

I want to delicate this to the ones that gave me the strength to follow through with my dreams. No matter what you come across in life, just strive to make it come true. Love yourself and keep the positive strong within and you will strive to living your dreams. I want to give a special thanks to Charles Thomas whom read my work and gave me the inner confidence I was lacking within so in order to be the woman I am meant to be, thank you with all my heart. To Calvin Burks for giving me the idea for Pink Lemonade.

Pink Lemonade

You say you want to taste some pink lemonade?
I am an original all homemade
So you have to hit the right signal
So I need you all big and tight
Because you never know I might bite
Just a little bit
Now don't sit, because you need all your whit
Or you might shit

So you want to taste some pink lemonade?
First I need you to suck my tit
Now don't give me any fits
Because I need to know if you can eat my clit

So you want to taste some pink lemonade?
This is so true, I won't taunt you
So don't get blue because I need you to eat my curly Sue
So I need you to stay on track
As you get ready to crack my back
Because now I am ready to hit the sack

You want to taste some pink lemonade?
Now if you move swift and fast you won't sink,. But we can be in sync
So don't blink, take a wink, and iron out all you kinks because we will
    find The right link

Now you want to taste some pink lemonade?
So I need you to be ready to baste me with your mouth that will set is
    both Free
With no time to waste, so put your hands at my waist and get ready
    to taste

Still needing to want some pink lemonade?
Time is moving and I need speedy because this is no treaty, because you
    know I have all your sweeties
So prepare for an unforgettable thrill
Because you might shrill, as I get to feel you
And there is no bill, as we seal the deal

So you want to taste some pink lemonade?
I took you from shrink to your brink of hardness
So as we clink, clink you don't know what to think
But when we are done you might need some first-aid

And I showed you that I am no Old Maid because you can't evade this
    pink lemonade
And as you stayed, touched, tasted, you can't evade or be afraid of this
    pink lemonade

Hot Sauce

Ready for some hot sauce?
You thought
You have caught
Sliding in the right slot
Putting us in a knot
Hitting my hot-spot/g-spot
While sampling the tea-pot
Still focusing on our train of thought
Blooming my flowerpot
As you continue tasting my hot sauce

Umm..Umm.. Hot Sauce
Don't forget to floss
You might feel cross
But moving softly across
With no kiss loss
Sliding side to side
As smooth as applesauce

Yes.. Hot Sauce
You have kissed off my lip gloss
As your hands crisscross
Making sure there is no smash lost
After you planned your path
That you have already sought to touch
Covering all the blind spots

Hot Sauce
Not time to jot
Placing me on your cot
That has brought

Us to a higher watt
Rocking back and forth like in a yacht
So follow your eye-shot
To firing up the jackpot

Keep on Tasting my Hot Sauce
Bleep, Bleep
Let's leap
As you peep
All over my humps
Reaching the heaps
Speeding the right gears of my jeep
To get ALL OF MY HOT SAUCE

Deeper, deeper
Sweeping passions limits
Smashing rations
With your counteractions
Crashing all the asking
Using your talent with what you imagine
Building traction
Outlasting to the ultimate end
As we bend, tend, send, and mend
defend, extend, to comprehend
To contend all the way
To the final end
Of finally tasting and eating all my hot sauce

Jelly Beans

I lick, taste, nibble the different flavors of Jelly Beans
Bursting from the seams
While stroking the limbs to make it to the stem
As the Jelly Beans starts to trimmer between my lips all wet and warm
What does this mean?
I take my dreams with my acquired Jelly Beans to the extreme screams
With my many mixed flavors of creams
That deems the steaming supreme pleasing both our needs
To each pleasures intense degrees as we feel and sees with the slickness
    of ease
Now lets get into it as I lick, taste, nibble the different flavors of your
    Jelly Beans
I like black, brown, pink, and white
So let's carry what what it is
And if we can make it out of my Chevy
Breathing heavy and especially as you burst like confetti
Singing like a Canary
You might see some fairies
As I hold softly tight to the Jelly Beans
Now you believe in my expertise that exceeds to what we agreed
But has passion pleasures guarantees
I have released and relieved and answered your pleads that brought you
    to your knees
You want appeals for more
As I tame the bouncing Jelly Beans
I think that you should not double think
Because I move quick as a blinking wink
Soft as mink, and having you moving to my tune in sync
Melting you in my mouth rink
Feeling the Jelly Beans harden
With your flipping belly

Eating you like I am at the deli
Have you reeling that leads to kneeling
Wheeling the dealing
No concealing while revealing
How much I love the different flavors of Jelly Beans
So let's keep you squealing while I am pealing
Each layer of you freewheeling
And finish with me sealing all your healing
Placing you on the absolute ceiling of climaxing release
With any flavor Jelly Beans

Hot and Sweet Coffee

Umm.. you are Hot and Sweet Coffee
With you having me with steamy thoughts
Starting me off with a wow jump start
That will have us both tied in knots
With you covering all my body's long shots

Now come on Hot and Sweet Coffee
I have you a sweet treat
Bring me your big hot meat
I'm ready to eat
Licking and nibbling to my heartbeat

Damn...Hot and Sweet Coffee
Trust and believe I will complete
I might just overheat
With you becoming to a prickly heat

So come on How and Sweet Coffee
Now I have you all saucy
With some softy rocky touching
As I become more naughty

I moan...Oh, bring it home My Hot and Sweet Coffee
Taking in all your raw stuff
Tasting all you hard stuff
Moving in hard thrusts as we get a little rough
I have you eating my favorite spots
As now we have swapped
Everything unlocked

Psat...Psat...Hot and Sweet Coffee

Don't become shocked
Because I have you twisted in knots
And now I have you propped
To be ready to be popped
So let's no impart
Because I need some more of your Hot and Sweet Coffee
Bring me to heaven my Hot and Sweet Coffee
Slipping and sliding increasing our passion heat
That has exceeded the preheat
Now we are almost to completion
Increasing all our repeats
Exploring new variety meat
All while I have you spread out softly in my satin sheets
With my knees up
You slowly sweep up
With your closeup
As you are moving to the checkup, and then do a backup
Me having your heads-up, not letting up
Because now you are exploding to a blow-up

Hot and Sweet Coffee, now push up,
Because I have a new line up
That starts at bottom's up
That will round up as I set up
How I taste, baste, touch, kiss, and eat you to melt like a buttercup

Ummm...Hot and Sweet Coffee
Now anytime you want to holdup
In my love cup
We can link up
With a hellacious wind up
Damn...Hot and Sweet Coffee

My Sugar Cookie

Hi, Sugar Cookie
Taking all in fully
I know you want to boogie
Working downward to my Missouri Cookie
All with my Sugar Cookie

No, this is not a quickie
Hugging all cushy
We doing hickies
While kissing every nooky
Umm...Umm Sugar Cookie

Moving all spooky
Because we feeling lucky
Licking all out goodies
Still with my sugar cookie

Would he
And would she
Could see
Then put me
As we should see
How sticky we can be
Umm...Sugar Cookie...Umm…

Not moving too prematurely
Touching all obscurely
Reassuring me
Minds all kooky
As Sugar Cookie eats my pussy

Now I know why
My Sugar Cookie has me high
As we reply to both of our supplies
I will not deny
Nor be shy
As you move up my thigh
We both imply and apply
Yes, Oh, yes Sugar Cookie

Now we comply
That is hereby
The cry
How we under-lye
We both hit the fly
Umm..Damn Sugar Cookie...Damn...Sugar Cookie...

Noe you have eaten your sugar pie
Nit saying bye
Being hot as July
You will move swift as a spy
As you put my ass on Rye
All in my.....
Oh, Sugar Cookie take me home

After you eat the whip foam
Sipping on the rum
No more alone
No more unknown
Because we have it each others throne
All set in stone

Umm...My Sugar Cookie

Stir My Chocolate

I say Umm...I stir my chocolate
Yes, Umm..Stir my chocolate

I will touch
Lick to nibble
Eat and ride till you feel it

As I taste each layer
And my chocolate starts to melt
I know he has felt
My tongue as it hits with chills like a taser

I say Umm...I stir my chocolate
Yes, Umm.. I stir my chocolate

Umm..Umm..I give sensation to my chocolate
As I have your body at a tremble
With my hands as soft as fur
I need you as you were
I say...Umm...Umm...I stir my chocolate

Woo, woo
I see you have gooses
As you eat my pussy
Now don't get woozy now
As you nibble on mu boobies

I say Umm..Umm..I stir my chocolate
Yes, Umm..Umm..I stir my chocolate

I will touch
Lick to nibble

Eat and ride till you feel it
Yes, Umm.. I stir my chocolate

As I get my socket in orbit
My rocket is ready
To unlock your locket
The private movie is about to begin
That will have us getting groovy to
Get ready to eat your smoothie
As we get all gooey

I have you as my display
So lets play
So I can convey what kind of foreplay
That I relay while moving like we are dancing Reggae
So start your stroking play because we are doing a two-way
So eat away as I hit your hide-away
Licking and nibbling all underway

I say Umm..Umm..I stir my chocolate
Yes, Umm..Umm..I stir my chocolate
Umm..Umm..Stirring my chocolate

This is at my time of day
Doing it my way, the right way
On any work day
As I take you to your favorite get-away
So okay
I laid my pathway to match your rhythm play
Hitting all your archways
As I have you ridding to your feel, it all the way, then as you are now
     my all you can eat buffet

I say Umm.. Umm..I stir my chocolate
Yes, Umm..Umm.. stirring my chocolate

I will touch
Lick to nibble
Eat and ride till you feel it
Yes, Umm..Umm.. I stir my chocolate

Caramel Chocolate

We have an unscheduled festival
Setting up our spectacles
Hoping you are durable
Eating everything wearable

Um..Um.. Caramel Chocolate
You are so adorable that is incurable
Taking our touches to comparable sensations
Reaching to intense transferable emotions
Hitting each other's decimals

As I moan Um.. Um.. Caramel Chocolate
I have you all for me accessible
Mixing our chemicals
Nothing hypothetical
Spreading plentiful
Kissing, nibbling, feeling steamy naked flesh,
And nothing unforgettable

Taking all our passion to toxic levels
Overflowing flawlessly
With each droplet
I now scream OH, MY CARAMEL CHOCOLATE

I feel you hot and ready to explode like a flaming comet
Clinging to me like a corset
Hitting each clit pocket and grinding the sockets
Rocking in every orbit

Moaning Um.. Um.. Caramel Chocolate
Now I isolate to formulate as my hips circulate

Calculating as you inflate all into my hotplate
Faster and faster penetrations so then you immaculate
Our union as you release inside me
I am still moaning Um..Um.. My Caramel Chocolate
And as we rest
I know I am blessed
You put me to the test
Where we both reached our quest
Not getting dressed
I place my hand on your chest and
Now I am abreast
Making sure everything we expressed is addressed
As I lick, taste, suck, nibble and feel
I digest, confessed on your necked flesh
Then we are now to reach the gold-crest
From mid-west, down-south, northwest,
Everything oppressed
I have reached my…..

Um..Um...My Caramel Chocolate

Put Me On 24/7

You say you work too much
I know this is true as such
I just want a little touch on your hot, big, swollen hutch
So put me on 24/7

Now I climb your tree of heaven
Sighing in seventh heaven
So if you prefer
There might be a blur
Because now I have you at a purr
Umm...put me on 24/7

As you now oversee
Touch curve to curve
We take a spur
Down to my honeybee
Yes, Oh yes, put me on 24/7

Now take your python
With my eyes on
You putting your smile on
As I just ride on...and on
Circles, tighten, lifting then deepening to DEEPENING
As you place me on 24/7

I do advise on that you let me thrive on
Moving upright and moving slightly on, then having you arise upon
As you might whiten as I take care of your bouncing icons
Taking you to the full light on as I am now on your 24/7

Now you raise your brow
As I have you ready to say a vow
Of you taking the plow
As you endow purring a meow
With the arouse I cleared your drought
As you say aloud
Damn, why did I wait to put you on 24/7

You don't have to shout
Umm...it is just in and out, up and down
Moving to the beats of flavors
Reaching to the highest routes
Exploding climaxes
You moaning, you will always be in my 24/7

Wet Ass Pussy (WAP)

Umm.. Wet ass Pussy
Now I bet
You think you are seeing my assets
Putting you in a cold sweat
So increase your mindset
As you get ready for my wet ass pussy

Come on I am dead-set
With no regrets
Because I want you to use your tongue like roulette
Oh, my wet ass pussy

Come here home to me to my class
I have no hall pass
As you then are putting your hands on my ass
Awhile sipping on your shot glass
Still trying to outclass
My wet ass pussy

Now understand fully
I want you to eat my cookie
And know I ain't pushy, so bring me all your goodies
And be down to boogie, because I have my mouth on your big hot toosie
Umm..my wet ass pussy

Woogie, woogie
As you seem to lure me
This could be what we could see
Rocking, slipping and sliding like the sea
Oh, have mercy, Umm..you have my wet ass pussy

WAP< WAP
Don't stop, I love you on top
Chop, chop I am now going to swap
Bang, Bang, nonstop you now have me in heaven shock

WAP, WAP
OMG, you have me now locked
Ticking me to the clock
Thrust, thrust
You have me walking the dock
Damn...I popped and then you dropped as you popped

Umm....Umm.... You have now had MY WET ASS PUSSY

Sweet Red Wine

You send me a tweet
That you have some sweet red wine
And that you have a special beat
For you hot, flaming dark meat
That is making it to my hot seat
Pushing to the up beats
Of penetrations, now keep up
Because the ejection seat is rubbing specific heat
Taking a sip of sweet red wine
I aim not to get ahead
As I slowly place the tip of you into my mouth
Then I break bread as I swallow your round head
That is thick, swollen, and thumping in anticipation
As I lick, suck, nibble, and eat, as you let me take the lead
With each thread I move a little widespread
And you say, OH GO AHEAD
Then we sip some more sweet red wine
It is time that we dine, and take the vine into a twine
All is fine because our bodies are all aline
As our hands design and define all that we have divine
Following each other's hairlines, with a high sigh
The headline is set all to the gold mine
Still sipping on the sweet red wine
Now sunshine I hit the bottom line, I can not draw a line
Because you are taking me to the finish line
And as you incline, to recline
We both hit that chime, that is now prime time
Feeling each enzyme half-full time, doing double time
And even overtime, while being perceptive with each reaction times

Almost to the end of the red sweet wine

Now come here to me anytime, to seek special time, at bedtime, because we can climb all the time, to have all the access time that we need when we both have the taste for some Red Sweet Wine.

Oh Dear Charles

Oh, Dear Charles,

This is to let you know that I am infatuated with your charms. But on some days you might snarl with just a touch of a brawl. But then you smile that brings me around a full mile. Then you lick your lips and I want a sip to taste your sweet luscious lips. And my mind is doing back flips wondering when we can touch.

Oh, Dear Charles,

You remind me of a soft chocolate bear, that has eyes to stare at and see through you, to really see you. That inner strength that can hold all on it's own, that brings you lifting my skirt, making it all clear. I say don't stop, because I want you to make me pop. Now we are only in first gear that will reach to high gear.

Oh, Dear Charles,

Our atmosphere is not going to disappear as you finally reach my lips to yours, then as my tongue makes it's way to your ear, you let out a soft moan. I whisper upon your hot flaming flesh, "Dear Charles". Now you have found your landing gear. No fear I have a hot sear you will feel.

Oh, Dear Charles,

The torture of waiting, the agony of anticipation, has led us to this uncontrollably sensation as our hands softly touch, looking, searching for hidden pleasures to the ultimate treasures. All the more we explore, you now have found my breasts and as you start to taste with your soft incredible lips, you lightly brush a nipple to nibble. And as I moan "Oh, Dear Charles" you brush the other nipple to nibble.

Oh, Dear Charles,

I can feel your body tense as I find your hard, swollen, hot ready manhood that now is in my hands. And as I stroke, I hear you moan against my breasts. Then I pull back for a bleak second, to now being my path of kisses and nibbles starting at your neck, and working my way to your nipples, all the way to your happy trail to my final goal. And then I take all of you into my mouth. I have found the treasures that I seek. And as I continue stroking, sucking, licking, with my tongue, and you feeling my tongue ring almost bring you to your peak. You lift me up and now we are eye to eye, and as you then lay me down and slowly enter me.

Oh, Dear Charles,

You stayed still for a minute that felt like forever then you looked into my eyes and started to move as I wrap around your waist as you slowly start penetrating me. Leaning down to kiss me on the lips, then my neck, to my breasts as my hands are now at your hips. Our hips moving in unison.

I moan, Oh, Dear Charles,

Then I turn and we roll and now you on the bottom. Hands clasped, I move ever so slowly. Rocking back and forth and then in little circles. I lift myself up where only the tip of your manhood is inside me. I then wait seconds and then take all of you inside me again. You now have a nipple in between your sexy lips, and on the other, so I can't lift up, so then I dig deep, and thrust harder and harder. Your hands move to my hips to help me thrusts. Then we both hit our release exploding into a million little pieces. I then lay across your chest to rest with you still inside me.

I say, Damn, OH, Dear Charles,
Oh, Dear Charles,

And then you grow hard inside me and wrestle the whole night through. Finding out each other's ultimate pleasures, with me moaning......

Oh, Dear Charles......

A Man Asked Me What I Need?

I am not only in need of a man's seed so get me a bead because I am a special kind of breed, so be ready to knead because I will have you ready to plead as we agreed I will tickle you like a centipede because you know I will succeed.

I am not any random chick, so choose your pick if you want to lick your wick of a dick, so with a quick click I will have you thick as a double quick as my lipstick is now gone and I am playing with your night stick creating my own picnic.

A man asked me what I am need of?

As you asked I will have my blast with nothing masked so put all in the past because I have you aghast now hold fast because you have not heard my whole forecast so as I can outlast while I have you as slick as glass and I will keep you flabbergast so leaving nothing unmasked.

A man asked me what I need?

So picking the right man will sometimes have you like a handy-woman wondering if he has the right sedan or van so scan the tan, hit to be overran and began your bran as you have him pull out his tin-can in the back of his mini-van, so ow I have begun my plan and eating my sweet pecan.

A man asked me what I need?

As I put you down on your knee and let you know I am your Queen Bee, I will tell you I now set you free with an unforgettable glee that now you can see I answered your plea and made you holler like a Banshee, so we are always carefree to a degree and this is a guarantee. I am now your sweet pea, and as you sip your tea by the sea there is no escapee because you are tied to my tulip tree.

Now I have answered the man whom asked what do I need.

Hercules

Hercules, you promised to show me some guarantees
That you have a unique was to succeed
To release your big thick machine
Bouncing into me like a trampoline

I believe in you Hercules
That your physique
Laying me on purple leaves
Respecting each others courtesies
As we encircle each...

Come to me Hercules
Hips moving in circular circles
Increasing our internal heat
Melting us together like cream cheese
We are both at ease
While we tickle the fresh breeze

Wow, Oh,,my Hercules
Our touches making a masterpiece
With each squeeze, I moan Oh, please
Stop the tease moving my knees
My body asking for sexual pleas
As your tongue is eating fast as bees to no degree

Oh, Hercules
Our orgasm is high as a trapeze
Stretched out thin as you freeze
Sliding into my hot ready melted cheese
You show me all your expertise

Umm….Umm.. Hercules
As I hit my release
You take me to the freedom of the seas
Me thinking we are complete

No, not you Hercules
Moving deeper and deeper
Meter by meters
Making me a squeaker
Rising higher our steamers

I can only moan, Oh Hercules
Be my teacher
Making me a believer
As we conquer our fevers

Oh, Damn, Oh, Hercules

Yum, Yum

Yum, Yum
You want me to eat your cum

As you smack your gums
Your beats hitting me hard like a drum
Then you sip your Rum
As you start to strike the thumb

Yum, Yum
You want me to eat your cum
Now you have to peak my cherry plum
Strum me dumb numb
Bringing me to succumb

As I say
Yum, Yum
You want me to eat your cum
As our mouths meet
We can't stand on our feet
Landing on the sheets
Hearing only our heartbeats

Yum, Yum
You want me to eat your cum
Now you are in my hot seat
Spicing up to reheat
Keeping nothing indiscreet
Nope nothing incomplete
As now your sausage meat
Sliding into my sugar beet
Taking your trick and treat

Yum, Yum
You want me to eat your cum
Making nothing obsolete
As we tear a sheet
Almost coming to complete
Oh, Yum, Yum
You want me to eat your cum
I take you my Boo
With every clue
As we both know your intense cue
Because we each move through
What we know is true
As we bring to, anew
All into

Oh, yeah, Yum, Yum
You want me to eat your cum
Whew, now I see what you was up to
Knowing nothing you say was not untrue
Because you know how to follow through
So let's dip into
Everything overdue
And look into whatever you can live up to
Because as you attend to, and stick to
We will always get to

Yum, Yum
You want me to eat your cum

Untouchable

When we met
Our plans were not yet set
I know you was taken
But by God you have me hormones a baking
And I really want you for he taken

Untouchable

You have a unique physique
Which I know you have a special technique
That can have me squeak like a freak

Untouchable

Knowing I can't, but if I could I would
And as you stood here on Elmwood
I speak no falsehood
Because I just want to please your manhood

Untouchable

You have me caught in a double dutch
So I image us together
Moving our friction clutch
Wait. This is too much

Untouchable

I just need a sexual trail
Up and down running miles
Praying with styles
That I have your smiles

Untouchable

Now I am willing and able, telling no fables
To have you up on the pool table
All playable because now I have you naked to your navel

Untouchable

No worries,
I am enabled
Just soaking up the appraisal
Because you know there is no betrayal
All I need you to do is slide into my cradle
Then I will need a jumper cable

Untouchable

When we met
I will bet, you didn't think I can make you sweat
Damn, you have me wet
As the sunset sets
And I will have no regrets
Because I have my mind set
And I will hit my winning number roulette
With you singing to the string quartet
And now the bouncing bet is
That after we have our passionate duet
You will be smoking an unforgettable cigarette

But for now you may be untouchable

Birthday Sex

No matter what day
My Birthday falls
I will have me some balls

So if it is Monday
That is the day you obey
Whatever my wish, and without any delay

Tuesday
You do all my favorite foreplay
Leading to you eating me like an all you can eat buffet

Now Wednesday
We do the hump hump
As you repeat yesterday
Taking off my new lingerie

Thursday
Is also my Holiday
Revving up my horny engine Chevrolet
Meeting you halfway

Opps Friday
It is serve me workday
As you are working and arching vertebrates

Umm....Umm.....Saturday
Moving gracefully as the Ballet
Knowing there is no leeway
As we slide into Sunday
We convey

That you drove down the right driveway
Grinding into me like Reggae
As you are blooming my bouquet
So how is my Birthday sex?
I have checked all your specs
With no objects
All intensifying effects
So what is next?
Do we reflect what is between our mindful decks?
Showing how we respect
With each peck our bodies are bucking for beckoning

Then we pillow text
Sliding and smacking middle sex

Come on Birthday Sex
Now I have my cake
That completing my entree
As you match play
Because my birthday is feast day
Filled with sex
Everyday.

Purple Thong

You said you was coming by wearing your purple thong
Now don't make me wait all day long
Singing the birdsong
So stop prolonging
As you come to me in your purple thong

Umm.Umm..Let's see that ping pong in that purple thong
And as we come along we begin to bong, bong
To that old drinking song

Now what's wrong?
I know you are hard, hot, thick, and strong
As we both play along
Now let's put that purple thong where it belongs

So you know I know each cubic foot
So you don't want to pussyfoot
As you imply to apply your personal input
Then you slide into the output motion
Using our creamy tasting lotions
Covering all images of our inflamed notions
Climaxing everlasting emotions
As you show your devotions
Spilling our love potion
As you hit your main promotion
All in your purple thong

Now let's see
Have you unlocked all my hidden keys?
Have you replied to my needy pleas?
Did you oversee every body part?

Did you hit all heated degrees?
If the answer is yes then you now have the code to my master key
Swimming in my wet sea
Climbing the spindle tree
All the way to the third degree
Sucking on my sugar snap pea
Setting us carefree
All from you surprising me with your purple thong

Now as I take hold of your dick
I place my lips to the tip
To smoothly lick, flick. And use my tricks
Making you all slick real quick
Having you hard as a brick
Pulling back on your control stick
With a hard tick
Making every touch last longer
With a few soft kicks
With you just bringing it on wearing your purple thong

Now we both are clinging, springing, singing. And swinging into the
      ultimate climax of sensations
As we both have bells ringing
From you just wearing your purple thong for me.

Just Sit On My Face

I place my trust
That you will wait to bust
Because we both discussed
Oh, How hard we are going to thrust

Just sit on my face

I will admit
I can't do a full split
I won't quit
Because I have the right bit that will hit

Just sit on my face

Now, Hon
Let's get it on
Thereupon
You begun to eat my pecan

Just sit on my face

Now I ain't dry
But at sky high
You hearing my cry
With the reply
You will not deny
As you spread my thighs

Just sit on my face

I embrace
As you move away my lace
With a swift grace
With each memory trace
Touching mt souls database
Everyplace

Just sit on my face

Tongue playing a relay race
Making my passion rising up the staircase
Shaking and shattering my orgasm vase
Over-shattering your first base

Just sit on my face

You made my gut flutter
Making us melt together like butter
As you make me stutter
A soft mutter
I bluster, what I think I can muster
As you began to pucker, and pucker
Changing my color
All because you are my LOVER

Just sit on my face

Eye Candy

You want me to bring out the brandy
Because you are now having moving handles
That is coming in handy
I have to ask why?
Because you have already put me on a high fly
With your hands on my thighs
Moving swiftly, I can not pry
As you have only on your black tie
Having my body ready to comply
As your mouth is doing a swing by
Moving from top to bottom
I can only express my out cry
Because you do not have no small fry
With all the extra supply
As whereby, you let out your war cry
Because we are doing our wild ride
You have me all tongue tied
I can not untie

I say come here eye candy
Whereby I will not stand by
But I will open your fly
To put your swollen pop fly
All into my pot pie
Now I do imply
This is all touch flesh
Where nothing is dry
And you might cry
As you hit the open sky
Taking that final sigh
Because you have applied

Leaving me all bone dry
So lets glorify
I do not take no goodbyes
Because you will come back to reapply
I have all your supply
Always on stand by
Come here Eye Candy
I have your Eye Crack
Because I can also crack that back
Remember when we are in the sack
I do not have small snacks
I will whack that ass
Placing my attack
All on your hot swollen stack
And bounce back
Then bring back
To bounce back
I draw back
Then I hit that come back
To where you will have to dream of that six-pack

Now Eye Candy
We have made our own soundtrack
Took off the tie
Took the throwback
Pleasured the smokestack
With no looking back

Whenever you are ready
Eye Candy/Crack

Freaky Richie Rich

Come here Richie-Rich
As we start getting cheeky
Now let's not rush as you get sneaky
Then as you start to kiss to nibble, I get squeaky

Umm...Umm.. Richie-Richie
You have me heating up
Using your nifty moving hands
Making me pitchy
I can feel your Biggie Dickie against my hot inner thigh reaching
    number five

Now Richie- Richie
I have an itch
That needs a twitch
Tasting and licking every nitch
Here you go taking down my barriers that have me unhitched
So when will you do a dip...switch
Throwing in your hidden touches with your wild pitch

Yum..Yum.. Richie-Rich
Damn...You hit a base hit
As you are playing with my clit
But I also have you ready to submit
Because I have you throwing a fit
As I start to eat you like a banana split

Now, now it's my turn
You are about to burn what you yearn
Have no concern
There is no return

Because your manhood is upturned
And as your Biggie Dickie slides between my soft sensitive lips
You now learn that this is your point of no return

Come on...Oh, come on
I have you at a hum ready to cum
I still strum you with my tongue, and thumb
As you then shift to slide right on into my Ruby Rich
What? Richie- Rich?

Bring it on, and bring me to our gold of riches
As you penetrate me with your rhythm
My hips following in sync
You best not blink as we hit the brink
Of your orgasms exploding and me moaning
Damn, Oh Damn Richie-Rich

Brian's Cock

Brian's cock
It is big, hard, what a woman wants?
Tick, tock, it's time to hit the clock
With his jock
After he has his pick of the flock
Now don't quack
As he knock, knock
Having you in shock
Because he can grow his stock
Have you changing colors like peacock
Breaking the time clock
Saying hell no to wedlock
But hitting all your wall rock
All with Brain's cock

He will sweet talk
Cut out small talk
Have you screaming in aftershock
So as he interlocks
Around the clock
He then sets you in electroshock
With Brian's cock

He will sweet talk
Cut out small talk
Have you screaming in aftershock
So as he interlocks
Around the clock
He then sets you in electroshock
With Brian's cock

Brian gives you a dandelion
Roars like a mountain lion
Have you dancing like a Hawaiian
All with Brian's cock

When he has you in airlock
You won't be able to walk
Think you are partying in Bannock
Rocking to bedrock
Sucking his ballcock

Covering all personal blocks
Being precise as a hawk
So don't mock
As he knocks you off your socks
All with Brian's cock

Now he has his sales talk
Using his authorized stock
Timing his grandfather clock
Taking his peck to the neck
Moving from low tech-to high tech
Covering the main deck
As he double check the upper deck
In a triple sec
All with Brian's cock

He says doll
Let's draw back to a crawl
As he placing his cue ball
Aiming for the wight ball
Having you eyeball
And hands on his meatball
Bearing all, covering all
All with Brian's cock

Chicken Wing

I call and ask if you are ready
Because I need my cuddle Teddy
As I know I make everything unsteady
But I am ready to make you some exploding confetti
So can you brings me your chicken wing
As I ping the king making you sing
Up to anything on the box springs

Wow, let me suck on the chicken wing
Sucking all the juices into my wet, warm, juicy mouth
Now things start to thicken and quicken
I have my vision of you snuggling like a kitten

Missing nothing as I am picking, licking, touching all forbidden
As you are having a battle of Britain
Because I have you living to listen
As I now have all your chicken wing in between my lips
Now there is things that brings us to our limbs entwined, bare skins
    sweating that has us all in spins
As you feel like you are floating at Colorado springs
Wait now my chocolate chicken wing
I have a new fast rate as you know this is fate
I move you to my satin plate
As you await I start to rotate
Also I liberate all of your chicken wing that I now have ready to erupt
    to a climax shatter
But before I allow...I raise my eyebrow as I slid you inside me
And you how I pow-wow
And as we are at the here and now
You tale me to chow chow
Oh, now you are my chicken wing

As I ride you astride
Take the glide eyes with pride
Because now you are all inside
Moving at low-tide to the joyride
Moaning alongside as I take you to yuletide
Just a little dignified as now I have clarified how I eat my justified
    chicken wing

Puerto Rican Spice

My Puerto Rican Spice
You came creeping one evening
Said you will take me to Eden
With your heart beating
We won't be sleeping

My Puerto Rican Spice
I don't do no cheating
If you are seeking what I have hidden that is sweeten
And as I make your knees weaken
You say you want to deepen

Oh, my Puerto Rican Spice
Let's just roll the dice
I know the price is nice
As you thrust twice
So with my advice you peek to entice
Have me seeing the Southern lights
As you now have me twisted in your elastic device

Now come here my Puerto Rican Spice
I will sacrifice as long as you are concise
Because now you have me twitching twice
As my body excites my hips hikes
So you don't have to improvise
My body sighs as you have now found my prize
As our eyes reunites
Our bodies passions cries
As your spread my thighs
Because you have taken me by surprise

Damn, My Puerto Rican Spice
As you eat your delights
I am here once, twice, and thrice
Taking me to where I am that ignites in snipes
I advise there is no revise
Because you have outline all that underlies
As our bodies complies

Oh, my Puerto Rican Spice
I hereby have you all dry
Always ready to reply to comply
Therefore you can't deny deny that I electrify
Because I am your butterfly

So come on my Puerto Rican Spice
You have hit the fireworks like the forth of July
With you singing a lullaby because you have the hook of the eye
So here we go my Puerto Rican Spice
All is now clear as you are now my dear all year
Because we said everything and left nothing unclear

Yes, My Puerto Rican Spice

Sensual Football

You have warm ups before the game, so as we stretch with a little bit of four-play to rev us up to be ready to play the game

So today I am ready for you to come play tackle football with me, so we might hot a wall, but I will have you standing tall, as I will show you all.

As you get in motion to tackle me, you now have heated up my emotions and they are locked in your chains of passion shackles, now you can see my forbidden freckles.

Now in football you have to hold onto the ball and I won't let myself fall as I look and hold on for the ride as you slide sweet and hot for the score (the touchdown).

We do have a lot of physical contact in football so be ready for me to smack your backside, because I have packed and made ready to be in motion for your hard stack, with your soft hands that have hit their mark at my kitty cat.

So now as we are sweating and heated from the game as we are slipping and sliding and our hands are holding strong, so we don't want to fumble as we hold our own, therefore not to get any interceptions, nor misconceptions of how to play football and of if you want a special exception you will just have to ask as I will take to salvation.

Now we have to cheer our fav team to have and victory so as we cheer. "Oh, yes, Oh God help me, yes right there, yes you have hit the spot, don't stop, and give me more, now you have a score!!!" We will relish in the passion united.

We try to keep score, and all in the same, but it is hard to remember who scored what, so it does not matter whom scores the most, but only how intense each one is scored.

Now we do have time outs and you get three per each half 30 seconds each, so which gives you enough time to catch your breath and plan on your next line of attack on each other's hot untouched places so thing of what you have already touched, so you can start on a new piece of hot necked flesh, as you kiss, nibble, taste, touch with a soft caress as you and I begin again.

Now not every time do we have overtime, but on special occasions it happens, so as we scored the same, now it is time to be extra creative in how we can make each other reach and extra climax, that will have you singing to the sounds of a sax.

As we have sent each other into the ultimate bliss our game has now come to an end so sleep and rest as you and we can be ready for the next game to come.

Sensual Basketball

Getting ready for the game can bring on a heavy workout, with stretching, softly touching to get the arousal of the opponent's attentions, setting up for heated passionate contact of the upcoming game.

The basketball game is about to begin and as you know the physical contact is very intense, with some quick surprising movements to throw the opponent off his game. And now it is time that we take our stance on the court, and I feel ready to take the incoming balls that is heading my way on full force, with anything the opponent is ready to strongly penetrate my waiting body.

The buzzard has went off and the game in now on and it will be on like cookies and cream with some Krispy Kreme on top. Now we have walked up to each other and now we are so close that our soft heated short breathing can be felt in the thick air as it is radiating off of our bodies that now has the waiting to an unnameable amounts of intensifying throbbing blood pumping. And our bodies automatically lean into each other that has an in visual pull that we both can feel with every bone in our bodies. Then our lips touch at a soft invitation, which you then came at me with your fast break move that you sweep me up off my feet and carry me to the gamepost and hold me up against the backboard fir support. All the while I can feel your hand making traveling movements, exploring farther and farther up my skirt, which now you have made one basket with your swish move that slithered in at my private net where you scored.

But I am on the fast move to counteract with me on the rebound move to now where I have you breathing harder and sweating, adding in my zone defense that is always at the ready and waiting. Knowing that it will help assist me when I get ready to box-out you, then to have you all drawn inside me moving at the pace I have set not allowing you to exceed me. But you are ready by sliding in your slick, hot, bug manhood of your hidden double dribble, taking your time having both of us moaning to your insane slow, sensual in and outs, that is about to take both of us home. And we both can feel the moving up and down, in and out, so slowly that I whimper to untameable passion and I can feel you tense and at the last second you reach down and take me home with you as we both make our basket.

And then you whisper the game is not over yet. I still have to use my backdoor. And as the words left your lips that is still upon my body feasting upon my harden nipples. I moan ready to take you all in again. The feel of you can not block out any area of the court that I have not traveled upon. I then have a move of my own as the ball is ow in my hand, I move swiftly to take my bank shot, that has helped you slide right back into my wet, hot basket. You then try to place a charge on me, but then my elbow gets in the way as we are moving again towards the center of the court. And therefore we move towards the key spot to make the free throw happen, that is when we take each other in our arms and place the lay-up move on each other bringing us closer and closer to my private basket that has landed us both ready for another score, and as we are nearing our peak moment you then want to do an alley-loop that has me all caught up in my exploration of your body that I seen not able to get enough of, and as this is now happening I am not sure how I will find myself landed. I am thankful that there was no air-ball in this game because I needed to feel every touch, kiss, hear our moans in unison, and mostly bring us both to fulfilling the frustration of our sexual pleasures of our personal basketball game.

Our game has now come to an end for now, but there is always a rematch in the waiting that we both can't anticipate the outcome of whom will ever win.

Printed in the United States
By Bookmasters